TUTOR'S HANDBOOK

Steven J. Molinsky
Bill Bliss

Contents

How to Be an Effective English Language Tutor

This **Tutor's Handbook** will teach you how to help young children develop reading and language skills using the materials in the **Word by Word Primary** program.

The **Word by Word Primary Phonics Picture Dictionary** is a vocabulary development program that helps young children learn the English language and learn to read. It presents over 1000 words and pictures in simple, easy-to-use lessons.

The **Word by Word Primary Workbooks** contain reading, writing, and listening activities. They have simple instructions and a complete answer key. There are three workbooks for different levels of instruction: Kindergarten, Grades 1–2, and Grades 3–4. (The examples in this Tutor's Handbook are from the Kindergarten Workbook.)

This **Tutor's Handbook** has simple, easy-to-understand instructions for using the Picture Dictionary and Workbook. It is designed for parents and other adults who will tutor children at home, in school, or in the community. It is also designed for older children who will serve as reading partners or buddies for students in lower grades. Even if you are an English language learner yourself, you can be an effective English language tutor if you follow the suggestions in this Handbook.

Basic Teaching Strategies

A typical lesson in the Picture Dictionary has words and pictures, with an illustrated phrase or sentence at the bottom of the page. Here are some teaching strategies:

1. **Introduce the Lesson:** Use simple language to explain the purpose of the lesson. (For example, "In this lesson, we're going to learn words that end in *ig*.")

2. **Present the Words:** Have the child look at the first word. Say each sound separately and have the child repeat. (Say the *sound* the letter makes, not the letter's name.) Say the word slowly and have the child point to each letter as its sound is heard. Then have the child read the word aloud. Do this for each word. (In later lessons, it may not be necessary to say each sound separately.)

3. **Talk about the Pictures and Word Meanings:** Have the child describe each picture, and make sure the child understands the meaning of each word.

4. **Analyze the Words:** Have the child count and identify the separate sounds that make up each word. (For example, "This word has three sounds: /w/, /i/, /g/.")

5. **Make Sentences:** Have the child think of a sentence for each word. (You might want to write the sentences and use them for more reading practice.)

6. **Read the Words in the Other Typeface:** Have the child read aloud the words on this line to practice reading this style of text.

7. **Spelling:** You can have the older child practice spelling the words in the lesson.

8. **The Illustrated Phrase or Sentence:** Have the child look at the illustration and talk about it. Read the phrase or sentence slowly and have the child point to the word as it is heard. Then have the child practice reading aloud. Finally, have fun with the illustration! Have the child suggest what the characters are thinking or feeling, predict what will happen next, or tell a story based on the illustration.

Additional Teaching Strategies

Rhyming Words lessons

(pages 56–59, 98–101, 140–141, 178)

Each of these lessons contains rows of pictures. All three pictures in each row rhyme.

1. Have the child look at the first row of pictures, say the words, and notice how they rhyme. Do this for each row.
2. Ask questions based on the rhyming words. (For example, "What rhymes with *can*?" or "I'm thinking of a word that rhymes with *dig*.") Then have the child ask *you* some questions.
3. For writing practice, the child can write the words and underline the letters that make the words rhyme.
4. Optional: The child can use the words to create sentences or even a poem. Write down what the child creates and use this for more reading practice.

Changes in Words lessons

(pages 60–62, 102–108, 142–144)

These lessons help children identify how words change when letters change. Each row is a separate exercise.

1. Have the child look at the first row of pictures and say the words.
2. Ask about the pictures in the first row. First, ask how the word on the left changes to the word in the middle. Then, ask how the word in the middle changes to the word on the right. For example:
   - A. How do we change *mat* to *map*?
   - B. Change the *t* at the end of the word to *p*.
   - A. And how do we change *map* to *cap*?
   - B. Change the *m* at the beginning of the word to *c*.
3. Repeat Steps 1 and 2 for each row of pictures. (You or the child might write the words as you do the exercises to help identify the changes.)

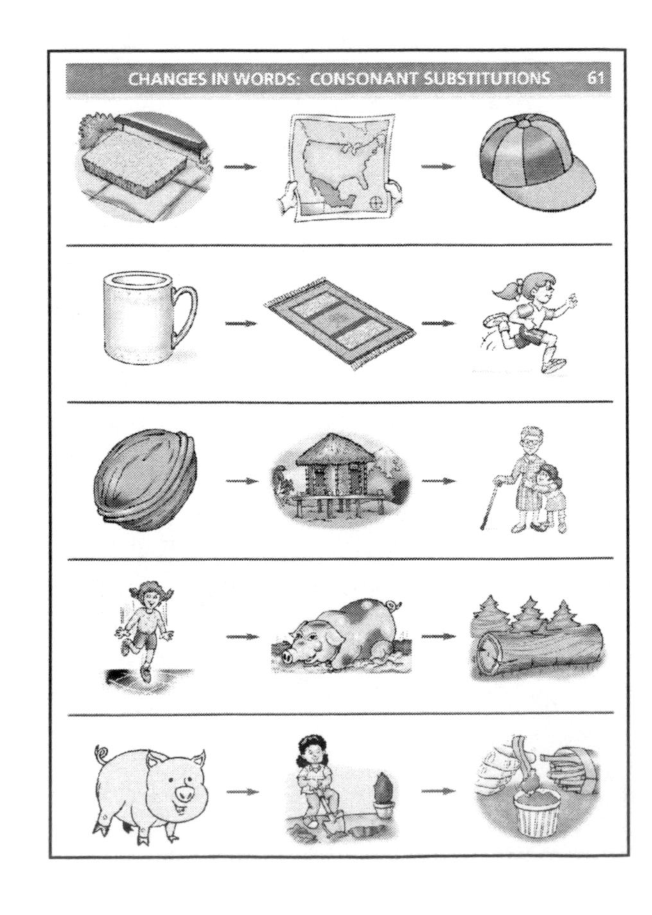

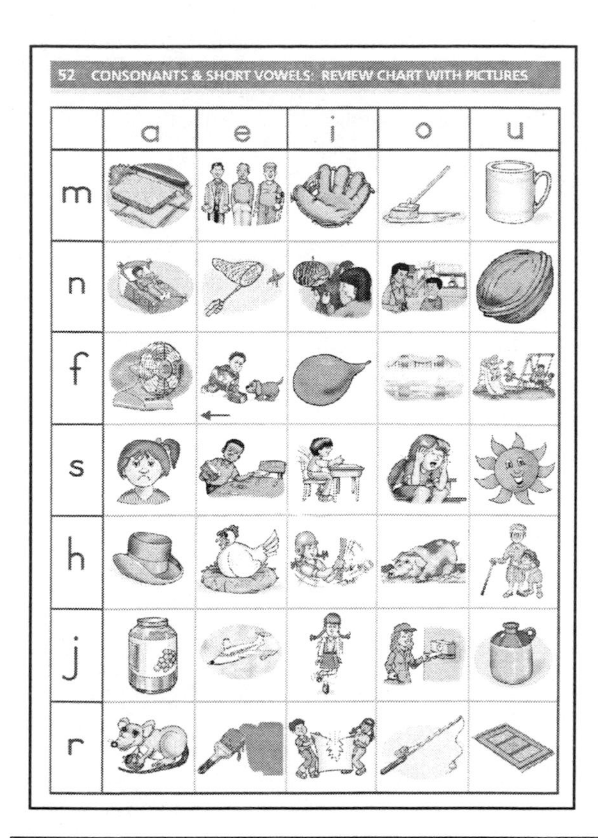

Charts

(pages 52–53, 96–97)

These lessons review vocabulary and skills.

1. Have the child say the words on the chart, reading from top to bottom and from left to right.
2. Point to any picture on the chart and have the child say the word.
3. Ask questions about the words. (For example, "What word starts with the letter *m* and has the letter *o* in it?" or "What word has the sound /r/ at the beginning and the sound /u/ in the middle?" Then have the child ask *you* questions.
4. You can also use the words for spelling practice or for making sentences.

Special Instructions

Pages 2–5: You can use the alphabet song to introduce or review letters.

Page 6: Say the places on the page, and have the child point to them (top, bottom, left, right, letter, word, sentence).

Page 37: Explain that the letter *a* sometimes doesn't say its name, but instead makes a different sound. Say the sound of short vowel /a/ and have the child repeat. Then say each word and have the child repeat (*add, ant*). Do this for the other vowels on the page.

Pages 92–95: Explain that these lessons practice identifying sounds at the beginnings and ends of words. For pages 92–93, ask questions such as, "Which word has the sound /m/ at the beginning?" or "Which word has the sound /m/ at the end?" For pages 94–95, first have the child identify the words and fill in the sounds. Then ask similar questions.

Pages 118–119: Have the child say each pair of words on page 118 and identify how the words are different. Then have the child identify the words on page 119 and write them in the book or on a separate sheet of paper.

Pages 156–161: Explain that longer words can be broken up into parts called "syllables." As you do these lessons, help the child identify the consonant(s) in the middle of words and the vowels on either side of the consonant(s).

Page 168: Point out that the plurals are in three groups based on the pronunciation and spelling of their endings.

Pages 172–173: Use sentences to practice the words in each column. For example: "Every day I *cook*." "Every day my friend *cooks*." "Yesterday I *cooked*." "Right now I'm *cooking*."

Pages 180, 182–187: Numbers in red indicate the pages on which the words first appeared. If the child can't read a word, go to that page for more practice.

Pages 189–191: For additional practice, say different words and have the child give the synonyms or antonyms.

Pages 198–200: To practice these words, play the word game on page 200. Take turns asking the questions.

Pages 201–230: This "A to Z Picture Dictionary" is a special extra section the child can use to practice the vocabulary.

Workbook Activities

Suggested strategies for using the Workbook:

Exercise instructions appear as easy-to-understand symbols. (The symbols are explained in English at the back of the Workbook and in Spanish on page 13 of this Tutor's Handbook.)

To use the **listening exercises**, read from the listening scripts at the back of the Workbook. (A complete answer key is also at the back.)

LISTENING: INITIAL SOUNDS

DICTIONARY page 14

1.

2.

3.

4.

5.

30

WRITING & READING PRACTICE

DICTIONARY page 22

fan
pan — pan

man
ran

can
van

tan
can

ran
van

fan	fin	run	ran	ten	tan
Dan and Jan ran in the hot sun.					

54

The child can do the **written exercises** with you during the tutoring session. Or, have the child do them alone, and then go over them with you. Have the child read aloud to you all words in all activities in the Workbook.

The **reading activities** contain words from current and previous lessons. Have the child read aloud to you these words and sentences.

(The Kindergarten Workbook has activities for Picture Dictionary Units 1 and 2 and pages 74, 80, 180-185. The Grades 1–2 and Grades 3–4 Workbooks have activities for the entire dictionary.)

Glossary of Key Terms / Glosario de términos básicos

adjectives adjetivos

alphabet alfabeto

antonyms antónimos

changes in words cambios en las palabras

colors colores

common irregular sight words palabras irregulares reconocidas a la vista de uso frecuente

complex word families familias de palabras complejas

compound words palabras compuestas

concepts about print mecanismo de la lectura

consonants consonantes

consonant blends combinación de consonantes

consonant digraphs dígrafos de consonantes (dos consonantes que representan un solo sonido, ej, *ch*)

decoding and word recognition decodificación y reconocimiento de palabras

distinguishing diferenciación

double consonants consonantes dobles (ej, *ll*)

final final

homophones homófonos

identifying and classifying objects cómo identificar y clasificar objetos

inflections inflexiones

initial inicial

irregular plurals plurales irregulares

living things seres vivientes

long vowels vocales largas

medial medial (letra o sonido en medio de una palabra)

multiple meaning words palabras con varios significados (homónimos)

multisyllabic words palabras multisilábicas

nouns sustantivos

phonograms fonogramas

plurals with spelling changes plurales con cambios de ortografía

r-controlled vowels vocales delante de la letra "r"

regular plurals plurales regulares

review chart tabla de repaso

rhyming words palabras que riman

root words palabras de las que se derivan otras

shapes formas

short vowels vocales cortas

silent letters letras mudas

simple prefixes prefijos simples

soft consonant consonante suave

sound/letter association asociación de sonido y letra

sounds sonidos

spelling changes cambios de ortografía

suffixes sufijos

syllabication división de las palabras en sílabas

synonyms sinónimos

two-syllable words palabras de dos sílabas

vocabulary vocabulario

vowels vocales

vowel digraphs dígrafos de vocales (dos vocales que representan un solo sonido, ej, q<u>ue</u> = e)

vowel diphthongs diptongos

vowel sounds and spelling patterns sonidos vocálicos y patrones ortográficos

word palabra

word family familia de palabras

***y* as a vowel** "y" como vocal

Enseñe inglés de manera eficaz

El **Manual del maestro particular** le enseñará a cómo darles clases individuales a niños de edad preescolar y los primeros grados de la escuela primaria para que desarrollen las habilidades de lectura y lenguaje utilizando los materiales del programa **Word by Word Primary**.

El **Diccionario fonético ilustrado Word by Word Primary** es un programa de desarrollo de vocabulario que ayuda a que los niños aprendan el idioma inglés y aprendan a leer. Presenta más de mil palabras e ilustraciones en lecciones sencillas y fáciles de entender.

Los **Libros de actividades Word by Word Primary** contienen actividades de escritura, lectura y comprensión oral, con instrucciones sencillas y claves para comprobar las respuestas. Hay tres libros de actividades para diferentes niveles de instrucción: preescolar, 1º y 2º grado, y 3º y 4º grado. (Los ejemplos presentados en este manual han sido tomados del Libro de actividades del nivel preescolar).

El **Manual del maestro particular** contiene instrucciones sencillas y fáciles de entender para utilizar el Diccionario ilustrado y el Libro de actividades. Se diseñó para padres y otros adultos que se propongan enseñar a niños en sus hogares, escuelas o en la comunidad y también para niños mayores que sirvan como compañeros de lectura a estudiantes de grados inferiores. Incluso si usted también está aprendiendo el idioma inglés, podrá convertirse en un maestro particular eficaz si sigue las sugerencias que le da este manual.

Estrategias de enseñanza básicas

Una lección típica del Diccionario ilustrado contiene palabras e ilustraciones acompañadas de una frase u oración con una ilustración al pie de la página. Algunas estrategias para la enseñanza son:

1. **Introduzca la lección:** explique el propósito de la lección con claridad y sencillez. (Diga, por ejemplo: "en esta lección vamos a aprender palabras que terminan en *ig*").

2. **Muestre las palabras:** enséñele al niño la primera palabra. Diga cada sonido por separado y pídale al niño que lo repita. (Haga el *sonido* que hace la letra; no diga el nombre de la letra). Diga la palabra lentamente y pídale al niño que señale cada letra a medida que vaya oyendo el sonido. Después pídale que lea la palabra en voz alta. Repita este procedimiento con cada palabra. (Más adelante quizás no sea necesario decir cada sonido por separado).

3. **Hable sobre las ilustraciones y los significados de las palabras:** pídale al niño que describa cada ilustración y asegúrese de que él entienda el significado de cada palabra.

4. **Analice las palabras:** pídale al niño que cuente e identifique los sonidos separados que forman cada palabra. (Por ejemplo: "esta palabra tiene tres sonidos: /w/, /i/, /g/").

5. **Componga oraciones:** pídale al niño que piense en una oración para cada palabra. (Usted puede escribir las oraciones para utilizarlas posteriormente como práctica de lectura adicional).

6. **Lea las palabras impresas en el otro tipo de imprenta:** pídale al niño que lea en voz alta las palabras de esta línea para que practique la lectura de este tipo de imprenta.

7. **Ortografía:** usted puede pedirle al niño, si es de un grado más alto, que practique deletreando las palabras de la lección.

8. **Frase u oración ilustrada:** haga que el niño mire la ilustración y comente sobre la misma. Lea lentamente la frase o la oración; pídale que muestre las palabras a medida que las vaya oyendo. Después deje que practique leyendo en voz alta. Al final, ¡diviértanse con la ilustración!: hablen sobre lo que crean que los personajes están pensando o sintiendo, traten de adivinar lo que pasará a continuación o pídale al niño que invente un cuento basado en la ilustración.

Estrategias de enseñanza adicionales

Lecciones de palabras que riman

(páginas 56–59, 98–101, 140–141, 178)

Cada una de estas lecciones contiene filas de ilustraciones; cada fila tiene tres ilustraciones que riman.

1. Pídale al niño que mire la primera fila de ilustraciones, diga las palabras y note la rima entre ellas. Haga esto con cada fila.
2. Hágale preguntas sobre las palabras que riman. (Por ejemplo, "¿qué rima con *can*?" o "estoy pensando en una palabra que rima con *dig*"). Después deje que el niño sea quien le haga las preguntas a usted.
3. Para practicar la escritura, el niño puede escribir las palabras y subrayar las letras que hacen rimar las palabras.
4. Opcional: el niño puede emplear las palabras para hacer oraciones o incluso un poema. Anote lo que el niño haga y empléelo para hacer prácticas adicionales de lectura.

Lecciones de cambios en las palabras

(páginas 60–62, 102–108, 142–144)

Estas lecciones ayudan a que los niños identifiquen cómo cambian las palabras cuando las letras cambian. Cada fila es un ejercicio aparte.

1. Pídale al niño que mire la primera fila de ilustraciones y diga las palabras.
2. Pregúntele sobre las ilustraciones de la primera fila. Primero pregúntele cómo cambia la palabra de la izquierda a la palabra del medio y después pregúntele cómo cambia la palabra del medio a la palabra de la derecha. Por ejemplo:
   A. ¿Cómo cambiamos *mat* a *map*?
   B. Cambia la *t* que está al final de la palabra a *p*.
   A. ¿Y cómo cambiamos *map* a *cap*?
   B. Cambia la *m* que está al principio de la palabra a *c*.
3. Repita los pasos 1 y 2 para cada fila de ilustraciones. (Usted o el niño pueden escribir las palabras mientras hacen los ejercicios para identificar los cambios).

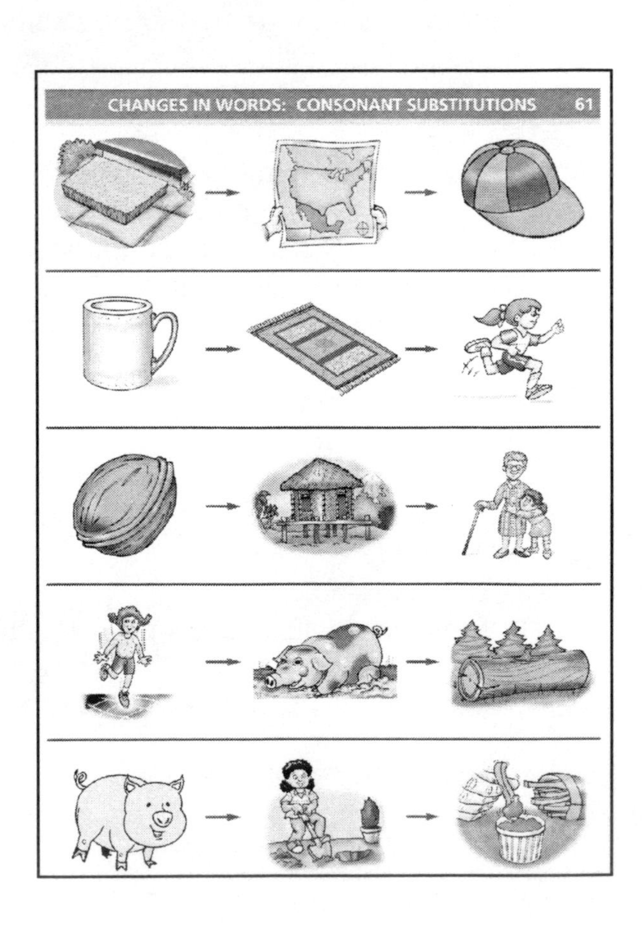

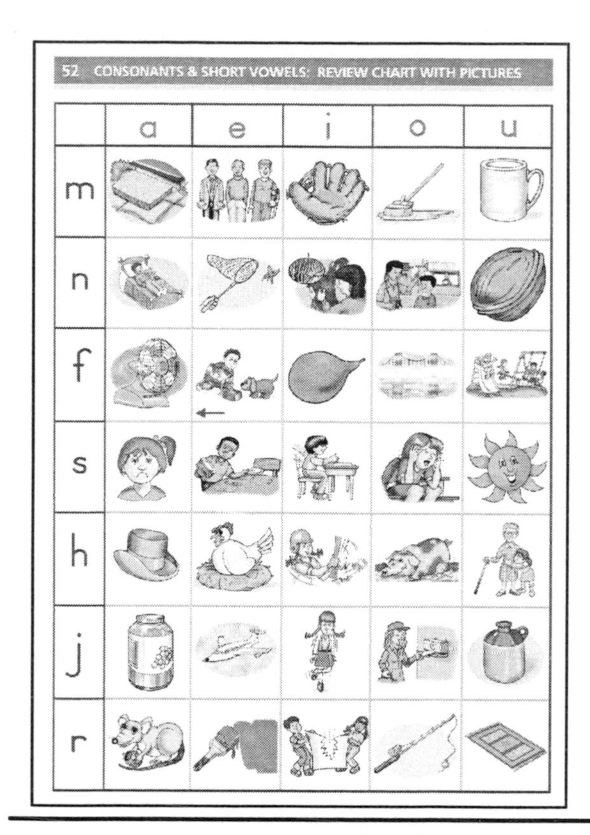

Tablas

(páginas 52–53, 96–97)

Estas lecciones repasan vocabulario y habilidades.

1. Haga que el niño diga las palabras que están en la tabla, leyendo de arriba a abajo y de derecha a izquierda.
2. Señale cualquier ilustración en la tabla y pídale al niño que diga la palabra.
3. Haga preguntas sobre las palabras. (Por ejemplo, "¿qué palabra comienza con la letra *m* y contiene la letra *o*?" o "¿qué palabra tiene el sonido /r/ al principio y el sonido /u/ en el medio?"). Después deje que el niño sea quien le haga las preguntas a usted.
4. También puede utilizar las palabras para practicar su ortografía o para hacer oraciones.

Instrucciones especiales

Páginas 2–5: usted puede usar la canción del alfabeto para presentar o repasar las letras.

Página 6: nombre las partes de la página y lo que hay en ella y pídale al niño que lo señale (parte superior, pie de página, izquierda, derecha, letra, palabra, oración).

Página 37: explíquele que a veces la letra *a* no se pronuncia como su nombre, sino con un sonido diferente. Pronuncie el sonido de la vocal corta */a/* y pídale al niño que lo repita. Después pronuncie cada palabra y haga que el niño la repita (*add, ant*). Haga esto mismo con las otras vocales que aparecen en la página.

Páginas 92–95: explíquele al niño que estas lecciones sirven para practicar cómo identificar los sonidos que están al principio y al final de las palabras. Para las páginas 92 y 93, haga preguntas tales como "¿cuál palabra tiene el sonido /m/ al principio?" o "¿cuál palabra tiene el sonido /m/ al final?". Para las páginas 94 y 95, haga primero que el niño identifique las palabras y escriba los sonidos. Luego haga preguntas similares.

Páginas 118–119: pídale al niño que diga cada par de palabras de la página 118 y hágale identificar las diferencias entre ellas. Después pídale que identifique las palabras que aparecen en la página 119 y escríbalas en el libro o en una hoja aparte.

Páginas 156–161: explíquele que las palabras más largas se dividen en "sílabas". Al hacer estas lecciones, ayude al niño a identificar la(s) consonante(s) en el medio de las palabras y las vocales de ambos lados de la(s) consonante(s).

Página 168: señale que los plurales están en tres grupos dependiendo de la pronunciación y la ortografía del final de las palabras.

Páginas 172–173: utilice oraciones para practicar las palabras de cada columna. Por ejemplo: "Every day I *cook*". "Every day my friend *cooks*". "Yesterday I *cooked*". "Right now I'm *cooking*".

Páginas 180, 182–187: los números impresos en rojo indican las páginas donde aparecieron las palabras por primera vez. Si el niño no puede leer alguna palabra, vaya a esa página para más práctica.

Páginas 189–191: como práctica adicional, diga palabras diferentes y pídale al niño que diga los sinónimos o antónimos de las mismas.

Páginas 198–200: para practicar estas palabras, hagan el juego de palabras que está en la página 200. Hagan las preguntas por turnos.

Páginas 201–230: este "A to Z Picture Dictionary" es una sección especial adicional que ayudará al niño a practicar el vocabulario.

Actividades en el Libro de actividades

Estrategias para utilizar el Libro de actividades:

Las **instrucciones para los ejercicios** aparecen como símbolos fáciles de entender. (Los símbolos se explican en inglés al final del Libro de actividades y en español en la página 13 de este manual).

Para utilizar los **ejercicios de comprensión oral**, lea en voz alta las transcripciones que se encuentran al final del Libro de actividades. (Allí también encontrará una clave completa para comprobar las respuestas).

El niño puede hacer los **ejercicios escritos** con usted o si prefiere, pídale que los haga por sí mismo para después revisarlos juntos. Haga que le lea en voz alta todas las palabras de todas las actividades del Libro de actividades.

Las **actividades de lectura** contienen palabras de las lecciones corrientes y de las previas. Pídale al niño que le lea en voz alta dichas palabras y oraciones.

(El Libro de actividades preescolar contiene actividades para las unidades 1 y 2 y las páginas 74, 80, 180 a 185 del Diccionario ilustrado. Tanto los Libros de actividades de 1º y 2º grado como los de 3º y 4º grado contienen actividades para el diccionario completo.)

CLAVE DE INSTRUCCIONES PARA EL LIBRO DE ACTIVIDADES*

	Lea (en silencio y en voz alta). Practique individualmente, con un compañero/a y con la clase.
	Trace.
	Escriba.
	Trace y después escriba.
o	Seleccione la respuesta correcta (ponga un círculo o un óvalo alrededor de la misma).
	Seleccione la respuesta correcta y después escriba la palabra.
	Escuche y seleccione la respuesta correcta.
	Escuche y ponga una marca debajo de la ilustración correcta. Después, escriba una palabra para cada ilustración que haya marcado.
	Ponga una "x" en la ilustración que no pertenece al grupo.
	Trace una línea que una la ilustración de la izquierda con la palabra correcta de la derecha.
	Escriba cada palabra de la casilla bajo la categoría correcta.

Permita que los niños escuchen y digan todas las palabras de todas las actividades de este libro. Los niños pueden hacer las actividades en silencio en la escuela o en sus hogares y entonces practicar las palabras en voz alta ya sea en la clase, con otro niño o con un maestro particular, ayudante, un padre u otro adulto.

* Workbook Activity Instructions Key (appears in English on last page of Workbook)

PICTURE DICTIONARY ANSWER KEY/ CLAVE PARA EL DICCIONARIO ILUSTRADO

Pages 52–53

See words on pages 54–55.

Page 56

can	fan	pan
pig	dig	wig
hot	pot	cot
map	tap	lap
wet	jet	net

Page 57

rug	tug	bug
hat	bat	cat
pet	vet	set
cut	nut	hut
sip	zip	rip

Page 58

fig	jig	big
pad	dad	sad
bun	sun	run
pop	hop	mop
tub	cub	rub

Page 59

wag	bag	tag
hog	log	fog
hen	ten	pen
pit	sit	hit
ham	yam	jam

Page 60

pin	pan	pen
hat	hit	hot
pit	pot	pet
bug	bag	big
jig	jug	jog

Page 61

mat	map	cap
mug	rug	run
nut	hut	hug
hop	hog	log
pig	dig	dip

Page 62

pop	mop	map
rip	rap	tap
jet	net	nut
hog	fog	fig
bug	beg	bed

Page 92

milk	drum
sand	glass
band	tub
ten	spot
nest	skin
pink	ship

Page 93

fox	cliff
gift	frog
lamp	bell
desk	sled
king	stick
chess	bench

Page 94

box	cub
gull	flag
pond	drop
dust	shed
mask	swim
can	truck

Page 95

fast	huff (or puff)
lift	smell
net	can
sink	dress
shell	dish
think	math

Page 96

math	mend	milk	mop	mug
nap	nest	nit	nod	nut
fast	fell	flip	fox	fun
sack	set	sick	sock	slug
hand	hen	hill	hog	hunt
jam	jet	jig	job	jump
raft	rest	ring	rock	rug

Page 97

lamp	left	list	lock	lunch
band	bend	bib	box	bump
plant	press	print	pond	puff
drank	dress	drink	doll	dust
track	tent	trick	trot	truck
glass	get	gift	got	gull
camp	Ken	cliff	clock	crust

Page 98

camp	lamp	stamp
nest	west	vest
kick	sick	pick
lock	clock	block
jump	hump	bump

Page 99

class	glass	grass
mix	six	fix
dent	bent	tent
sand	stand	band
yell	tell	sell

Page 100

chin	win	thin
path	bath	math
sing	king	ring
pitch	itch	switch
tank	bank	thank

Page 101

mash	crash	trash
sack	black	track
sting	sling	swing
duck	luck	truck
hill	spill	quill

Page 103

ill	hill
ring	bring
fog	frog
sing	sting
bank	blank
chip	chimp

Page 105

stick	tick
trot	tot
slip	sip
tent	ten
drink	rink
quilt	quit

Page 106

left	lift	gift
hand	band	bend
patch	pitch	ditch
tank	bank	bunk
fish	dish	disk

Page 107

ship	shop	chop
chin	chick	sick
stop	step	stem
shell	spell	spill
slip	skip	skin

Page 108

sing	sting	sling
blank	bank	back
sang	sand	stand
wink	wing	swing
sack	sick	stick

Page 119

can	cane
kit	kite
cub	cube
pin	pine
cap	cape
cut	cute

Page 140

train	plane	rain
boat	coat	note
spoon	prune	tune
throw	hoe	blow
pool	stool	mule

Page 141

road	toad	rode
snow	toe	bow
glue	new	threw
skirt	hurt	shirt
zoo	blue	you

Page 142

rake	cake	cane
bite	bike	hike
fly	fry	cry
mice	rice	race
car	card	yard

Page 143

sleep	sheep	sweep
short	shirt	skirt
ate	gate	gave
cape	tape	tap
man	mane	plane

Page 144

sea	seal	meal
row	crow	grow
tub	tube	cube
flute	cute	cut
harp	sharp	shark

Page 178

long	song	wrong
trash	splash	mash
knock	lock	sock
door	pour	store
straw	draw	saw
dome	comb	home

Word by Word Primary Tutor's Handbook

Pearson Education
10 Bank St.
White Plains, NY 10606

ISBN 0-13-022199-6
Printed in the United States of America

10 9 8 7 6 5

Editorial directors: *Allen Ascher, Louise Jennewine*
Director of design and production: *Rhea Banker*
Associate director of electronic publishing: *Aliza Greenblatt*
Production manager: *Ray Keating*
Senior manufacturing manager: *Patrice Fraccio*
Manufacturing buyer: *Dave Dickey*
Electronic production editors, page compositors, interior designers: *Wendy Wolf, Paula Williams*
Cover designer: *Merle Krumper*
Cover artists: *Richard E. Hill, Carey Davies*
Illustrations: *Richard E. Hill, Maya Shorr Katz*